Nicki Greenberg

PICTURES BY Nicki Green[berg]

IT'S TRUE!

Squids Suck

ALLEN&UNWIN

First published in 2005

Allen & Unwin
83 Alexander Street
Crows Nest NSW 2065
Australia
Phone: (61 2) 8425 0100
Fax: (61 2) 9906 2218
Email: info@allenandunwin.com
Web: www.allenandunwin.com

National Library of Australia
Cataloguing-in-Publication entry:

Greenberg, Nicki.
It's true! squids suck.
Includes index.
For children.
ISBN 1 74114 627 5.
1. Cephalopoda – Juvenile literature. I. Title.
594.5

Series, cover and text design by Ruth Grüner
Cover photographs: Thomas Burch (squid Iridoteuthis iris)
and Australian Picture Library/© Dennis Blachut (octopus arms)
Set in 12.5pt Minion by Ruth Grüner
Printed by McPherson's Printing Group

1 3 5 7 9 10 8 6 4 2

**Teaching notes for the It's True! series are available
on the website: www.itstrue.com.au**

CONTENTS

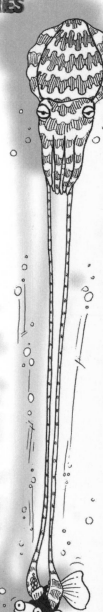

Why squids?

The truth is, I wasn't planning to write a book about squids at all. My big idea was to write a fascinating, fast-paced book about my favourite animals – snails.

The problem was that every time I opened a book to study those snails, I was distracted. I couldn't stop reading about their amazing cousins, the cephalopods. It was hard to keep my mind on snails when all around me there were tales of giant squids, brainy octopuses and shape-shifting cuttlefish.

Finally I had to admit it – snails may be beautiful, but compared to squids they lead pretty quiet, dull lives. So I left the snails to destroy our garden in peace, and dived into the extraordinary underwater world of cephalopods. It's been quite an adventure – I'm so glad I did!

Michael Greenberg

News flash!

Mysterious eight-armed stealth hunters are prowling the planet!

From their ocean stronghold, the jet-powered shape-shifters have delivered their warning:

'WE ARE EVERYWHERE!'

But what exactly are these creatures
– and why can't we find them?
Our snorkelling reporter came back
with nothing more than a squirt
of ink in the face. Who can solve
this deep-sea mystery?'

It's true! From tropical beaches to the icy Antarctic depths, squids and their relatives really are everywhere. In fact, they take up more space on the planet than humans!

So how come these suckers are so difficult to spot? Why do they boggle biologists and puzzle predators?

Here's your chance to enter the bizarre world of cephalopods and find out.

In this book, you'll discover some of their best-kept secrets. You'll have a close encounter with the vicious Jumbo Flying Squid, play hide and seek with the super-smart Mimic Octopus, be hypnotised by a cuttlefish, and look into the biggest eye on the planet . . .

Think you can handle it? Then strap on your scuba gear and get ready to see some really great stuff – and some really gross stuff too. One thing's for sure – you'll never look at calamari the same way again . . .

1

MEET THE FAMILY

Squids are part of the group of animals called cephalopods ('*kef*-a-lo-pods', or '*sef*-a-lo-pods' in the USA). Cephalopod is Greek for 'head–foot', because their 'feet' seem to grow straight out of their heads. Actually, cephalopods don't have feet like other animals – they have arms which grow out from around their mouths. You could say that their arms are really super-lips or that their mouths are in their armpits!

Other cephalopods include the super-stretchy **octopuses**, the very colourful **cuttlefish** and some really ancient creatures, the **nautiluses**.

Cephalopods are part of a larger group of animals called molluscs. Their mollusc relatives include land snails and slugs, oysters, clams and a whole lot of other soft, slimy, squishy things that you wouldn't want to step on.

To help you recognise your new cephalopod buddies, the pictures on the next page give you an example of the basic, common shapes of an octopus, a squid, a cuttlefish and a nautilus. There are many variations on these shapes.

SQUID

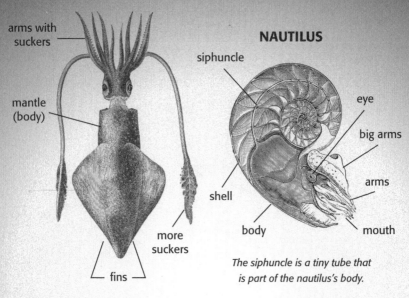

arms with suckers

mantle (body)

more suckers

fins

NAUTILUS

siphuncle

eye

big arms

arms

shell

body

mouth

The siphuncle is a tiny tube that is part of the nautilus's body.

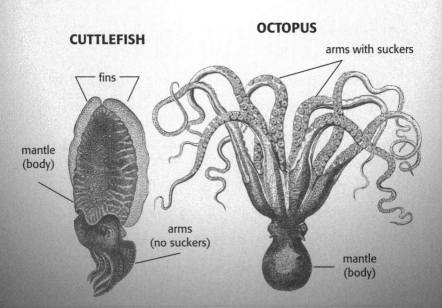

CUTTLEFISH

fins

mantle (body)

arms (no suckers)

OCTOPUS

arms with suckers

mantle (body)

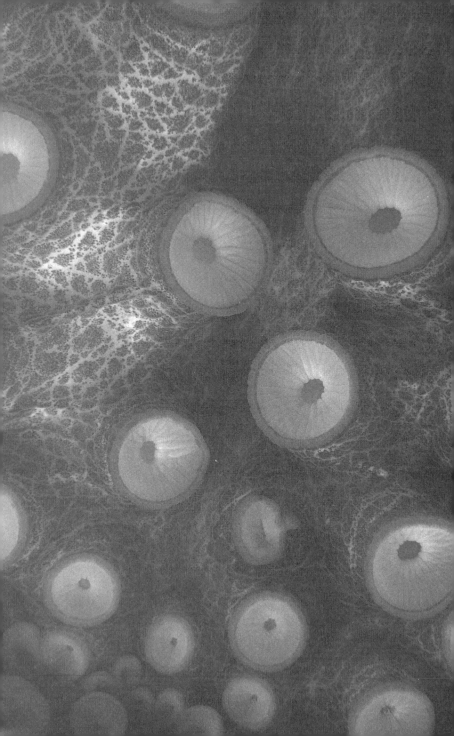

Humans have discovered over 1000 different species of cephalopods so far, but there are surely more to come.

Scientists have worked out that squids alone have now overtaken humans in their 'total biomass'. This means that squids now take up more space on the planet than humans. Luckily for humans, cephalopods only live in the oceans and haven't conquered the land . . . yet!

Cephalopods live in all waters of the world, from shallow rock-pools to the darkest, most mysterious ocean depths. They come in all sorts of shapes, colours and sizes, from the size of a five-cent piece to 18 metres long – longer than a bus!

Cephalopods are the most intelligent of the molluscs, with the most complex bodies and brains. Octopuses are especially smart. In fact, some scientists believe that octopuses are as intelligent as dogs.

If that sounds impossible, read on. You're in for quite a few surprises . . .

2

BLUE BLOOD AND BRAINY ARMS

Get a grip!

The most obvious weird feature of an octopus is its eight arms. In this book you'll discover a lot of bizarre things that octopuses can do with all those arms – like carry home the shopping, unwrap a clam sandwich and even do a bit of home renovation.

11

One of the secrets of these tricks is the octopus's suckers, which you can find on the insides of its arms. These suction-cups are smooth and bouncy but very strong. An octopus can use its hundreds of suckers like fingers, co-ordinating them to perform delicate and complicated tasks like pulling the meat out of crab legs. They can even open screw-top jars!

Squids and cuttlefish can't do quite as much with their arms, but they do have some extra surprises up their sleeves. As well as the standard eight arms, they have two long feeding tentacles which are specially developed to shoot out and grab prey.

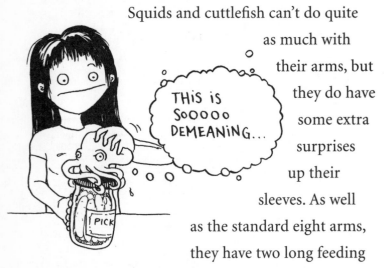

Once a squid has seized its prey, there is very little chance of escape. Squids' arms are also equipped with hundreds of powerful suction-cups, and once they get a

grip, they're very hard to remove.
Some of the bigger squids have hard,
spiky saw-teeth or hooks around the
rims of their suckers which hook into
the flesh of their prey. As some unlucky
divers have discovered, being cuddled
by a big squid can be a painful experience.

Being a smart-arms

The extraordinary thing about
octopuses' arms is that they're
super-strong *and* super-smart.
You're wondering how arms can be
smart? Well, think about this: humans
have only two hands, but even so it can
be hard to control both of them when
they are doing different things at once.
For example, try writing your name
with one hand and drawing a smiley face
with the other hand at the same time.
Not so easy, is it?

13

Now imagine that you have six more arms.
And all of them can bend, twist, curl and stretch
in any direction, without bones or joints limiting
that movement. So you have *millions* of choices of
which way to move. And instead of ten fingers, you
have maybe 1500 sucker discs to co-ordinate. Your
brain would be working overtime to direct all those
complicated movements.

So how do octopuses do it? The answer is that the
octopus's brain doesn't have to think about all the
movements of each arm. The detailed instructions for
those movements come from the arms themselves.

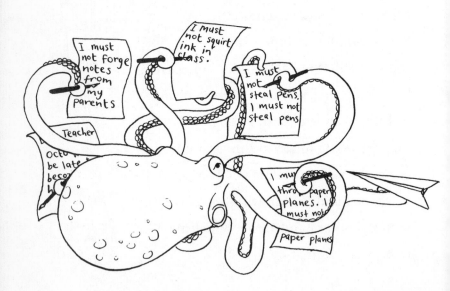

Each arm has a sort of 'mini-brain' – a bundle of nerves that directs the arm to move in special patterns. So the octopus only has to think of the general thing it wants to do, and the arms automatically do the rest. If an octopus's arm is torn off in a fight, the arm can keep moving and grabbing even after being disconnected from the body because its mini-brain keeps on giving it instructions. Even better, the octopus can grow a whole new arm to replace the lost one, complete with a new mini-brain.

Mighty muscles

Octopus arms are not only smarter than human arms, they're also a lot stronger. If a strong person tries really, really hard, they can drag an object that is about double their own weight. But an octopus can drag an object that is *20 times* its own weight! So the Giant Pacific Octopus, *Octopus dofleini*, weighing up to 150 kilograms (330 pounds), could pull something as heavy as a car. And all this without any bones in its body at all. Impressed?

GIANT PACIFIC OCTOPUS
(*Octopus dofleini*)

Imagine an octopus that could open the bonnet of your car with one arm while closing the boot with another. Impossible? Not if you live in the sea off British Columbia, Canada.

This is the home of the world's biggest octopus, the Giant Pacific Octopus. With an arm span reaching up to 4 metres (4 yards plus), this shy creature is longer than a caravan, and very strong.

In nearby Seattle in the 1960s, divers used to compete to see who could find the biggest octopus, bring it to the surface and then wrestle it. This cruel 'sport' was no fun for the frightened octopuses, who would struggle with the divers in the water and sometimes try to pull off their masks.

Strangely enough, the bigger octopuses get, the less fierce they are. So although these octopuses were much stronger than the humans who intruded into their world, the eight-armed giants soon gave up the fight when captured.

Who are you calling soft?

About 350 million years ago, the ancestors of today's cephalopods all had shells. These enormous creatures – like a 5-metre (5-yard) nautilus – were the master predators of the sea. Most cephalopods today have no outer shell, but the ancient nautilus still carries its beautiful orange-and-white spiral home. Sadly, humans are now threatening the existence of these 'living fossils' by catching them for their shells.

Cephalopods do not have any bones at all. They are invertebrates, which means 'without a backbone'. But they're not completely soft. Cuttlefish have a light, chalky shell inside – you may have seen them in budgie cages. This 'cuttlebone' is made of hundreds of tiny layers containing gas and liquid, which help the cuttlefish float. Squids have a gladius, which looks like a strip of plastic inside their bodies, but is actually a thin shell.

BUT i HATE SEAFOOD –

Most octopuses have no shell, and this allows
them to stretch and squeeze their bodies through tiny
holes and cracks. A 20-centimetre (8-inch) octopus can
squeeze itself through a hole the size of a 10-cent piece!

There is one part of a cephalopod's body that
is particularly hard. If you were to look inside a
squid's mouth (that's right, in the armpit), you'd find
something very sharp, very tough and very surprising
– not teeth, but a beak! Cephalopods have a strong,
curved beak like a parrot's, and believe me, you don't

RAM'S HORN SQUID
(*Spirula spirula*)

Have you ever found a delicate spiral
shell like this on the beach? If you look
closely, you will see that the shell is
made up of many closed chambers, and
the only way in is through a tiny pinhole.

This curly shell belongs to the tiny (6-centimetre
or half-inch) Ram's Horn Squid, and is *inside*
the squid's body. By adjusting the volume of
gas and liquid in the chambers of the shell, this
cigar-shaped squid can float or sink to different
depths. The squid will always float with its head
pointing downwards because the shell is in the
back part of its mantle (body). The mantle is also
decorated with a large, glowing light.

If you hold a delicate Ram's Horn shell too tightly,
it will shatter in your hand like glass. But when
the living squid fills the shell with water, it can
withstand enormous pressure. Ram's Horn Squids
have been found at depths of 1–1½ kilometres
(up to 1 mile), where the force of the water
pushing on the shell is more than half a tonne.
That's like having a great big cow stepping on
this little shell!

want one to bite you. Inside the beak is a radula ('*rad*-you-la') – a sort of hard, raspy 'tongue' covered with pointy 'teeth' like a file. Want a kiss, sweetheart?![1]

Blue-bloods

Cephalopods are the kings and queens of the mollusc class, not just because of their amazing strength, brilliant brains and jewel-like colours. Cephalopods actually do have blue blood! The chemical in their blood that carries oxygen is called haemocyanin ('*hee*-mo-*sy*-a-nin') and is based on copper. This copper pigment gives cephalopod blood its bluish-green colour. Human blood is based on an iron pigment called haemoglobin ('*hee*-mo-*globe*-in'), which makes it red.

The bad news for cephalopods is that blue blood might be prettier, but it's not very efficient at carrying oxygen to their muscles. Even though cephalopods

[1] If you want to get straight into the gory details about what cephalopods can do with their beaks, go to chapter 7. But don't read that chapter at night!

have three hearts pumping blood around their bodies, they still get tired very quickly and have to rest after each burst of activity. This means that every movement is important. If a squid doesn't successfully escape from a predator on the first try, it will be too tired to keep swimming away. And then it's *Goodbye, sucker!*

SNAP!

FLASH

CLICK!

THiS "ROYALTY" JOB SUCKS!

21

3

HAND IT TO ME, BABY!

Cephalopods pack a lot into a very short life.
The largest one, the giant squid, probably only lives
for about five years. An octopus rarely lives for more
than ten years. And throughout their short, colourful
lives, cephalopods are always at risk of being eaten by
predators. This might not sound like a program for
survival, but they do have a great way of keeping their
numbers up. When cephalopods have babies, they
don't just have one or two – they have thousands or
sometimes millions at once.

How do you like your eggs?

Cephalopod eggs can be smaller than grains of sand or as big as ping-pong balls. They can hang from rocks in lacy  frills, drift in the water like strings of beads, or stick out from the sea floor like bunches of flowers. Some have even stranger shapes – the eggs of the nautilus look like steamed dim sims! Many octopuses protect their eggs until they hatch, but most squids and cuttlefish leave their eggs and never see their young. Just as well, really, because many of their young will not survive.

The most risky time of any cephalopod's life is just after it hatches from its egg. A tender baby squid makes an easy snack, even for a very small fish. So when the babies hatch, many of them are quickly

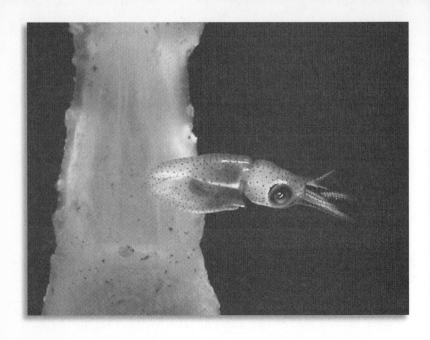

gobbled up. From the thousands or millions of eggs, only a small number of the babies will survive to adulthood.

Some cuttlefish have a clever trick for protecting their eggs from predators. They mix ink into the outer layers of their eggs. This black coating tastes nasty and is difficult to digest. Only the sea-star, which can eat just about anything, is able to digest these inky cuttlefish eggs. Of course, once the baby cuttlefish hatch, their protection is over.

Pass the parcel

Cephalopod breeding is weird in many ways. In all cephalopods, the male hands over a parcel of sperm to the female, and she uses the sperm to fertilise her eggs. But there are different ways of handing over these packets.

In many octopus species, the males have one specially shaped arm which they use for passing sperm packets to the female. The female then stores these packets until she is ready to use the sperm. Some female octopuses will store sperm for ten months before using it.

The Hooked Squid (*Chaunoteuthis mollis*) has a less gentle method of delivery. It uses hooks on its arms to make slits in the female's skin. Then it uses its penis to inject packets of sperm into the cuts. The female's skin grows over the wounds, so she can store the sperm to use later. No one knows how the female gets the sperm out of her skin to fertilise her eggs.

In some types of small squids, males will search the females for sperm packets left by other males.

They then scoop out the other male's sperm and replace it with their own.

I want to hold your hand . . . for ever

Mating is a deadly business for male argonauts. The argonauts are an unusual group of octopuses because the females have a delicate white shell. Male argonauts are much smaller than females, and they have no shell.

The male argonaut keeps his breeding arm curled up in a special pouch until he is ready to mate. Then he has only one chance

ACTUALLY, I'M NOT REALLY IN THE MOOD TODAY

to get it right. He loads the arm up with sperm packets, and says goodbye – to his arm and to his life. The arm breaks off, swims over to the female

and crawls into her body with its packets of sperm.
After losing his arm, the male argonaut quickly dies.

Very sneaky . . .

When cuttlefish mate, they make a real party of it.
In mating season, thousands of cuttlefish come
together for a frenzy of breeding. And in the confusion
of fighting for a partner and mating, all kinds of weird
things happen.

The Giant Australian Cuttlefish (*Sepia apama*) uses some especially cunning tricks during the annual mating frenzy. The sneaky ones are the smaller males, who would normally lose any contest with the bigger males. Taking advantage of the confusion, the smaller males change their body colour so that they look like females. Then, when the larger males are not looking, the little guys sneak up to the females, drop the disguise and quickly mate with them.

4

MOVE OVER, HOUDINI

It's not just their charming personalities and good looks that make cephalopods popular. Being soft, shell-free and very tasty makes them tempting snacks for underwater predators. But they've managed to survive by developing a whole range of escape tricks – including some really dirty tricks that leave Houdini for dead.[2]

---

[2] Harry Houdini was a famous American escape artist who could get out of just about anything: chains, padlocks, handcuffs. Pretty impressive for a human, but compared to an octopus he was nothing special.

zip!

It's a bird ... It's a plane ... No, it's Turbo Squid!

The simplest escape trick is to swim away as fast as you can. This is where the squids outclass the rest. When a squid really wants to *go*, it uses its muscular body (the mantle) to squirt water out through its funnel – a tube next to its arms. This makes the squid shoot backwards like a torpedo with its arms trailing behind. Cephalopods are the only creatures on Earth who move in this way. All cephalopods have funnels, and all use them to move around, but the others just can't beat the torpedo-shaped squids for jet-power.

SCOOT!

SHOW-OFFS

WHOOSH –

Some squids can even use their
jet-power to leap right out of the water.
These flying squids have specially shaped
fins and webs between their arms which help
them glide through the air. But this trick can
sometimes backfire: the squid might escape
from a hungry shark, only to be seized by
a squid-eating bird!

Hide and seek

ZIP!

Unlike squids, octopuses are pretty slow movers.
But when it comes to hiding, these guys are the
experts. Most octopuses love cosy spaces.
They can squeeze their stretchy, boneless bodies
through tiny cracks and holes and hide away
from predators in the most
unlikely spots.

WHIZZ

For example, octopuses are often found curled up inside old soft-drink cans!

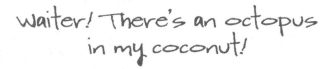

Some octopuses go one step further. If there are no ready-made hiding places available, they build their own houses, using pieces of rock, shell and other objects, and then barricade themselves inside. So what looks to you like a pile of rocks and rubbish may actually be an octopus's home. Once an octopus has built a house, it keeps the place tidy by sweeping the floor and pushing shells and food scraps out the door. Octopuses don't like to share their homes. Unlike squids and cuttlefish, they live alone.

Waiter! There's an octopus in my coconut!

What is the best part of a coconut? The sweet juice? Or the tasty white flesh? For the Veined Octopus (*Octopus marginatus*), the best part is the part that humans throw away: the hard shell. This octopus has discovered that old coconut shells make a perfect house.

In the shallow tropical waters around Indonesia, the Veined Octopus will dig around in the mud until it finds half a coconut shell that some human has tossed into the water. After cleaning out the mud with a few squirts from its funnel, the octopus will carry the shell on its suckers and go in search of another half. When it has found two suitable halves, the octopus can curl up inside and pull the lid shut. With its super sucker-power holding the two coconut halves together, the octopus creates a perfect fortress to protect it from predators.

Why don't archaeologists like octopuses?

To an octopus, a wrecked ship is like a five-star hotel full of fabulous hiding places. When archaeologists investigated the wreck of a 2000-year-old Roman ship near Marseilles, France, they discovered that the Common Mediterranean Octopuses (*Octopus vulgaris*) had moved in. This was great for the octopuses, who each had a perfect, custom-made apartment. But it was a major headache for the archaeologists . . .

The ship's cargo included many amphorae (Roman clay jugs for water, wine and oil) which had broken into pieces. There were also plenty of older Greek relics at the site, so it should have been an archaeologist's dream. But it turned out that the thousands of octopuses living there over the centuries had used the broken pottery shards and other objects to build their homes, and they were all mixed up. This made it

IF ONLY i HAD THE LAST PIECE! THIS RELIC WOULD BE PRICELESS...

extremely difficult to piece
the broken amphorae
together again and
work out the age and
origins of all the objects.

Even worse, over the years the octopuses had gathered
up *new* objects and mixed them in with the old ones.

. . . and is that a squid under the carpet?

Building (or digging up) a house isn't the only way to
hide, and sometimes even the simplest materials can
make great cover. For example, the Southern Dumpling
Squid (*Euprymna tasmanica*) has a really interesting
trick. It buries itself in the sand with only its eyes
showing. Then, if it wants to swim around, it can glue
sand onto its body, using a sticky substance which
oozes out of its skin. And if you disturb this squid, it
can release an acid from its skin, which un-glues the
sand. The falling coat distracts predators while the
squid makes its getaway.

All right — who inked their pants?

If you frighten a cephalopod, you may be in for a messy surprise. In one of the strangest escape tricks of the animal world, a frightened cuttlefish, squid or octopus will squirt a cloud of blackish ink out of its funnel. Before you can wipe the stuff out of your eyes, your eight-armed friend will have disappeared.

Baby squids are already equipped with working ink sacs. A newly hatched squid may only be a tiny 2 millimetres long (less than a tenth of an inch), but the first thing it does after emerging from its egg is shoot out a jet of ink. Squids grow very quickly, and they soon develop a powerful inking ability.

Cephalopod ink is made of highly concentrated melanin which is the pigment (colour) that makes some people dark-haired and dark-skinned. The melanin produced by cephalopods is so strong that just a few milligrams squirted out in a jet of water will form an impressive dark cloud. A cephalopod can adjust the direction of its funnel so that the cloud of ink shoots out between it and the predator. This distracts

the predator or acts as a
'smoke screen', giving
the cephalopod time to
change direction and escape.

Some of these inks contain
chemicals which irritate other
animals' eyes or interfere with their
sense of smell. The savage Humboldt Squid, which
you'll meet in chapter 7, has ink which is dangerous
to human eyes. Fishermen reeling in the jumbo squid
need to protect their eyes from the inky jets which the
huge squid pumps out with the force of a fire-hose.

Cephalopod ink doesn't dissolve in water. After a
short time, it turns into grey, cobweb-like threads that
drift in the water and snag on rocks.

To find out about some of the interesting ways that
humans use cephalopod ink, have a look at chapter 8.

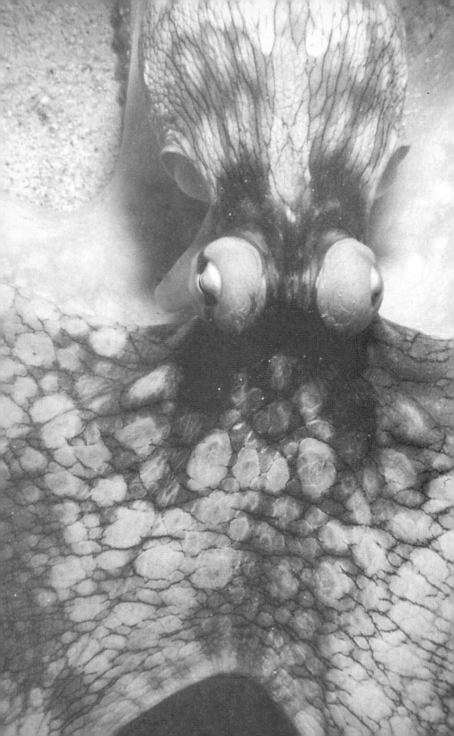

5

MASTERS OF DISGUISE

When you see squids or octopuses in the seafood section of the market, they usually have a whiteish, perhaps a mottled, pinkish-purple skin. Seeing them dead like this, you would never know that they were once brilliantly coloured shape-shifters. But it's true – cephalopods are absolute masters of disguise. They can change colour faster than any other animal on Earth and change their skin to look like rocks or coral. They can even disguise themselves as completely different animals. You think those chameleon lizards are impressive? Wait till you see this!

How do you make an octopus blush?

Camouflage is one of the cephalopods' most important survival tricks, especially for the slower-moving octopus. Even an octopus as big as the 10-kilogram (22-pound) Maori Octopus (*Octopus maorum*) can make itself invisible, by matching not only the colour but also the texture of the rocks and weeds around it. Like many other octopuses, it can change shape by raising knobbly spikes and bumps all over its skin.

Octopuses also change colour to show emotion, frighten an enemy and communicate with one another. Humans might blush when they're embarrassed, turn red with anger or pale with fright, but imagine if you showed your feelings by flashing blue spots or purple stripes all over your body!

The Red-spot Night Octopus (*Octopus dierythraeus*), which lives in shallow coastal waters around northern Australia, is one animal that makes no secret of its feelings. This 1½-metre (4-foot) octopus is usually a deep purplish-red colour with paler blotches.

But if it is frightened or disturbed, it will suddenly turn completely white with bright cherry-red spots and red eyes, in a display designed to scare off predators.

Cuttlefish steal the show

When it comes to colour-changing, the cuttlefish really steal the show. The Giant Australian Cuttlefish, for example, can switch instantly from a mottled orange and brown to a brilliant turquoise decorated with red and gold squiggles. It can even squeeze its skin into frilly green and yellow seaweed shapes.

Imagine this spectacular creature shimmering blue and green, purple and gold, with bands of darker colour pulsing along its body, over its rippling fins and down its curling arms. Now imagine this sight multiplied by a thousand, and you will have some idea of what cuttlefish mating season looks like off the coast of South Australia. Every year between May and August, thousands of these beautiful creatures gather to breed, putting on an amazing underwater light show with their mating and fighting displays. These animals really know how to dress for a date.

This extraordinary display is becoming a popular attraction for visitors, who can dive with the cuttlefish to get a close-up view. But the cuttlefish's life is both brilliant and short. After mating is over, the cuttlefish lay their eggs and soon die.

How do they do it?

The secret of cephalopods' amazing colour changes is in millions of tiny organs called chromatophores ('cro-*mat*-o-fours'). These are like little elastic bags of pigment (colour) all over the cephalopod's skin. Chromatophores are so small that more than 200 of them could fit onto one square millimetre of squid-skin. That means over 5000 chromatophores could fit onto your fingernail. And each one of them has a job to do.

Each of these microscopic bags is connected to a set of tiny muscles. When the muscles contract (tighten), they stretch the colour bag. As the bag grows bigger, more of its colour is visible. To create its magical multi-coloured patterns, a cuttlefish needs to control and co-ordinate millions of individual chromatophores, stretching and shrinking them at just the right moment and in just the right spot.

This is an enormously complicated task. It's a bit like trying to make every hair on your body stand up one by one – in height order. But the cuttlefish can do it in *two-thirds of a second*!

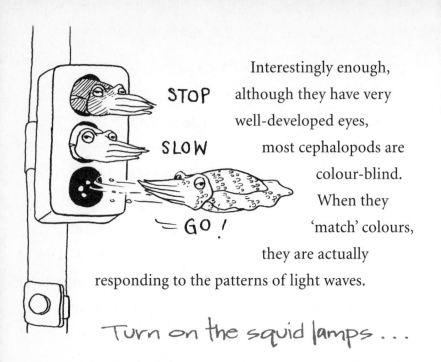

Interestingly enough, although they have very well-developed eyes, most cephalopods are colour-blind. When they 'match' colours, they are actually responding to the patterns of light waves.

Turn on the squid lamps . . .

Most cephalopods also have reflective cells called iridocytes ('i-*rid*-o-sites') which give their skin a green or blue metallic glitter. But some species go one step further. Instead of reflecting light, many squids actually make their own light.

Squids do not use their lights to see in the dark, but to make it harder for other animals to see *them*. Using a light to hide yourself may sound strange, but it is actually very clever. Predators on the sea floor can usually see a squid as a dark shape blocking out the light from above. But if the squid makes its own light, the predator looking up from below can't see the squid's dark shape, so the squid appears to be invisible.

There are some tricky techniques for making your body glow without using batteries. For instance, the Southern Dumpling Squid has a light powered by glowing bacteria. The Jewel Squid (*Histeoteuthis hoylei*) from Hawaii uses a different method. It makes its own light using chemicals called enzymes. This squid has another unusual feature – its left eye is always much larger than its right. It swims with the bigger eye pointed upwards, searching for the dark silhouettes of prey not lucky enough to have their own lights!

WHAT'S WITH THE SHADES, MAN?

I PREFER TO EAT IN THE DARK

FEATURE CREATURE
THE MIMIC OCTOPUS
(newly discovered species — no scientific name yet)

Imagine you are walking in Africa enjoying the sunshine and watching a herd of grazing zebras. Out of the corner of your eye you see a flash of tawny fur – it's a lion bounding straight at you!

Now imagine that you have an amazing secret power: by concentrating hard, you can squeeze your body into the shape of a poisonous cobra. The lion is almost on top of you – you can smell his rotten-meat breath in your face. But suddenly he leaps back. You look just like a cobra, and he's afraid of a deadly snakebite.

Handy trick, hey? Believe it or not, there is an animal that can do this: the extraordinary zebra-striped Mimic Octopus. Instead of hiding itself, the Mimic Octopus does something even more amazing.

It disguises itself as another animal – one that is poisonous, dangerous or nasty-tasting. Even better, the Mimic Octopus can choose just the right kind of disguise depending on which predator is nearby.

For example, if a damselfish is closing in, the Mimic Octopus can imitate a venomous banded sea-snake – a creature that eats damselfish. To do this, it buries six of its arms in the sand and gently waves two striped arms in the water like a snake.

To scare off other types of predators, the Mimic Octopus can stretch all its arms out like a flower, imitating the long spines

of the poisonous lionfish. Or it can flatten itself into a teardrop shape and take the form of the unpleasant-tasting banded sole.

The mysterious Vampire Squid (*Vampyroteuthis infernalis*)[3] has one of the strangest light tricks of all. This black, jellyish creature drifts a kilometre (more than half a mile) below the surface in almost total darkness. If a predator approaches, the vampire squid distracts it with glowing lights waving at the tips of its arms. Then the squid shoots out a sticky mucus containing thousands of sparkling, glowing spheres. While the predator is distracted by this light show, the vampire squid disappears into the darkness.

[3] *Vampyroteuthis infernalis* is Latin for 'vampire squid from hell'. This sounds scary, but the Vampire Squid doesn't really deserve its name. It may look frightening – like a black umbrella with its arms joined by capes of skin – but it is a shy, rather gentle animal.

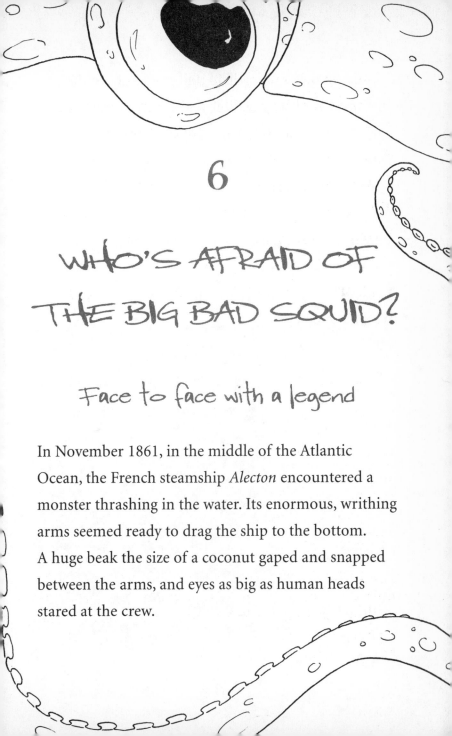

6

WHO'S AFRAID OF THE BIG BAD SQUID?

Face to face with a legend

In November 1861, in the middle of the Atlantic Ocean, the French steamship *Alecton* encountered a monster thrashing in the water. Its enormous, writhing arms seemed ready to drag the ship to the bottom. A huge beak the size of a coconut gaped and snapped between the arms, and eyes as big as human heads stared at the crew.

For centuries sailors had told stories about the legendary Kraken, a terrible sea-monster as big as an island, with arms as long and thick as the masts of a ship. The captain of the *Alecton* couldn't resist the opportunity to capture a Kraken of his own, and he ordered his men to shoot it with their muskets. The bullets seemed to disappear. Next they tried harpoons, but these glanced off the giant body. Finally, they managed to loop a rope around its tail and tried to haul the monster on board. It was much too heavy. The weight of the giant squid caused the rope to slice through its flesh, and the huge creature sank, leaving the captain with only part of the tail.

This fragment alone weighed about 20 kilograms (over 40 pounds). But the giant squid itself had disappeared, and the mystery continued.

Seven years earlier, a Danish zoologist called Jappetus Steenstrup had decided to challenge the fantastic stories about the Kraken. Steenstrup had studied the few scraps of evidence that were available, including the dried remains of an enormous creature owned by the king of Denmark. Steenstrup compared this creature with other smaller cephalopods, and concluded that it was in fact a giant squid. He named it *Architeuthis* ('ar-ki-*tooth*-is') which means 'ruling squid'. But in spite of this scientific evidence, sailors and fishermen preferred their terrible tales, and the legend of the Kraken continued.

The biggest mystery in the sea

More than 150 years have passed since Jappetus Steenstrup identified and named the giant squid. But this creature still remains the greatest mystery of the sea. No one has ever captured a live *Architeuthis*.

No scientist has ever seen one swimming in the sea, eating, mating or laying eggs. The giant squid is believed to grow up to 18 metres (20 yards) in length, including tentacles, and weigh about 250 kilograms (one-quarter of a ton). Yet it is so elusive that no one knows exactly where to find it. Not surprisingly, squid experts are in fierce competition to be the first to capture *Architeuthis* alive. But so far, despite all their expeditions, remote-controlled submarines and even 'critter-cam' cameras attached to whales, nobody has even come close. This gives you an idea of how little we actually know about the deepest parts of the ocean.

Giant squids probably live at depths of about a kilometre (over half a mile), and if they rise to the surface, it is usually because they are injured or dying. So we've learned about giant squids mostly by studying dead ones that have washed up on beaches. Over 100 giant squids have been found washed up

IT'S GOT TO BE DOWN HERE SOMEWHERE...

all over the world, but the 'hot spots' for *Architeuthis* seem to be New Zealand and Tasmania, where they have appeared as recently as 2004.

Don't mess with the big squid

Even a washed-up *Architeuthis* can be a powerful force, as a Newfoundland fisherman discovered in 1873. Seeing a giant squid in shallow water near the beach, the man rowed over to it and hit it with a boat-hook – a pretty silly move, when you think about it. Suddenly the enormous animal charged. It sank its beak into the wooden boat, wrapped an arm and a tentacle around it and began to drag it under. Luckily for the fisherman, he had a quick-thinking boy called Tom Piccot on board. Tom grabbed a hatchet and hacked off the squid's tentacle, freeing the boat. The squid shot out a great cloud of black ink and disappeared, leaving only the twitching tentacle. Tom was business-minded too: he sold the 5½-metre (19-foot) section of tentacle to the Reverend Moses Harvey, who later gave it to a museum.

FEATURE CREATURE
COLOSSAL SQUID
(*Mesonychoteuthis hamiltoni*)

Could there be a squid even bigger than *Architeuthis*? New Zealand squid expert Dr Steve O'Shea thinks so.

In 2003, fishermen in the icy Ross Sea, near Antarctica, found an enormous squid in their nets. They hauled it aboard and took it to New Zealand, where Dr O'Shea identified it as *Mesonychoteuthis hamiltoni* – the Colossal Squid. The squid was not fully grown, but already had a mantle (body) length of 2½ metres (8 feet), which is bigger than any *Architeuthis* mantle measured so far. Based on its mantle length, Dr O'Shea estimated that an adult Colossal Squid might be the biggest squid in the sea.

The captured squid's size was not its only remarkable feature. It looked like something out of a horror movie, with huge, rotating hooks growing from its suckers, pop-eyes and an enormous, sharp beak. The scientists concluded that the Colossal Squid was a fearsome predator, tougher and more aggressive than *Architeuthis*.

But would it really grow bigger than *Architeuthis*? This is a mystery yet to be solved.

Tasty but tough

Much of what we know about giant squids comes from studying the stomachs of sperm whales. The sperm whale is the only creature big, strong and toothy enough to eat fully grown giant squids, and captured whales often have many enormous undigested squid beaks in their stomachs. Sperm whales are big eaters – one whale was found with the remains of 18 000 squids in its stomach!

Architeuthis may be a tasty meal for a sperm whale, but it is not an easy one. The captured squid will fight, even as the whale chomps on its body. The squid's weapons are its arms, covered with saw-toothed suckers, which it wraps around the whale's head. Sperm whales often have round, sucker-shaped scars on their lips and heads from these dinner-time battles. Even so, the whale is much stronger and always wins.

JUST EAT iT, SON –
DON'T PLAY
WiTH iT !

Follow that spew

Just how much do giant squid researchers love their work? Enough to sift through a bath full of mucky, stomach-churning, stinky, *purple* whale vomit? You bet.

Prince Albert of Monaco was a keen naturalist with a particular interest in cephalopods. When he followed a whale-hunt in 1895, he saw a harpooned whale vomiting into the water. But instead of being disgusted, the Prince was delighted. What a great opportunity to study the giant squids that the dying whale had eaten!

In the hot, bubbling mess of whale spew, Prince Albert saw the bodies of several enormous deep-sea octopuses and squids. He realised that the whale must have eaten these giants very recently, as they had not yet been digested. With great excitement, he ordered his men to catch the bodies – along with plenty of lumpy, half-digested goo – in their nets.

The Prince and his team of assistants found some extraordinary things, including an immense squid whose suckers were covered with sharp claws. But to discover these treasures, the men had to sift

through what Prince Albert described as 'a purple mass, in full fermentation, littered with eyes and beaks which had resisted the action of the gastric juices'. The stench of this disgusting mixture ended up making many of the crew vomit as well.

Some scientists have even stranger methods of collecting giant squid beaks. One squid expert puts on his scuba diving gear and goes swimming behind sperm whales, catching their poo in a butterfly net! How many people do you know who would risk being pooped on by a gigantic whale in the hope of finding some squid beaks?

Now *that* is dedication to your work!

TRUE OR FALSE?
GIANT SQUID TRIVIA

THE ANSWERS ARE ON THE NEXT PAGE, BUT TRY TO GUESS – YOU MIGHT BE SURPRISED!

❶ Giant squid eggs are the size of ostrich eggs.

True ☐ False ☐

❷ *Architeuthis* has the biggest eyes of any creature on the planet.

True ☐ False ☐

❸ *Architeuthis* is the biggest animal in the world.

True ☐ False ☐

❹ *Architeuthis* are rough when mating.
True ☐ False ☐

❺ A giant squid can stop a yacht by grabbing onto it.

True ☐ False ☐

❻ *Architeuthis* is a powerful, fast swimmer.

True ☐ False ☐

❼ Calamari rings from a giant squid could feed a family for six months.

True ☐ False ☐

ANSWERS

❶ FALSE.
Giant squid eggs are very small. A newly hatched *Architeuthis* is about the size of a cricket! To reach its huge adult size, *Architeuthis* needs to eat large amounts regularly.

❷ TRUE.
At 25 centimetres in diameter, the eyes of *Architeuthis* are the biggest on earth. Like other cephalopods, the giant squid has very good vision.

❸ FALSE.
The blue whale is the biggest animal. But the giant squid is the biggest invertebrate (animal without a backbone).

❹ TRUE.
The male giant squid injects sperm packets into the female's skin using his penis like a nail gun.

❺ DEPENDS WHO YOU BELIEVE . . .
In 2003 the French racing yacht *Geronimo* mysteriously came to a halt in the middle of the Atlantic. The crew reported that when they looked into the water, they saw an 8-metre giant squid wrapped around the hull and pulling on the rudder. When the crew stopped the boat, the squid disappeared.

❻ FALSE.

Architeuthis is not a sprinter. It is more of
a gentle cruiser, and probably gets tired quite easily.

❼ YOU DECIDE!

If you chopped up the body of a giant squid, you'd
have calamari rings the size of truck tyres. But would
you really want to eat them? The giant squid's flesh
contains a lot of ammonia, which helps it to float
(ammonia is lighter than water). So if you like the taste
of floor-cleaner, you might enjoy a meal of giant squid!

I'M NOT SO SURE
ABOUT THIS
ARCHITEUTHIS
CALAMARI....

7

FEEDING FRENZY

So far, cephalopods probably seem pretty friendly.
OK, the giant squids might sound like a bit of
a handful, but on the whole they look like cuddly
little critters, right? If a cute little Striped Pyjama
Squid followed you home from the beach, you'd want
to keep it, wouldn't you?[4]

Well, this chapter might just change your mind.
Now you're going to see cephalopods at their most
cunning, their most dangerous and most aggressive.
Because now it's *feeding time* . . .

[4] Don't try this. Cephalopods hate being kept as pets and most
don't survive in captivity. For a photo of a Striped Pyjama
Squid, turn back to page 7.

Before we set out on a little hunting trip, let me remind you about the eating equipment hidden in the middle of all those arms. That's right, the powerful parrot-like beak – very hard, and very sharp. And inside the beak, there's that rough, rasping radula, like a little chainsaw ready to shred the food and shovel it down. With a mouth like that, who needs a knife and fork? Or teeth?

Squid attack!

Speed and accuracy are the trademarks of a squid attack. Squids usually eat fast-moving prey like fish or other squids (even squids of the same species –

look out, bro!), and this requires special hunting skills. Like other cephalopods, squids have very good eyesight which they use to pinpoint the location of their prey.

Catching the prey is the trickiest part, and this is where the two extra-long feeding tentacles come in. The ends of these tentacles are shaped like a leaf and covered with strong suckers, and the squid can shoot them out with surprising speed to snatch moving prey. The Giant Squid has an extra, unique feature. Its feeding tentacles can zip together to form one long club with metre-long grabbing 'tongs' at the end.

Once the squid has reeled in something tasty, the other eight arms do their job, wrapping around the prey and holding tight with their hundreds of suckers. All this happens very quickly. Within seconds the squid will snap the fish's spine with its curved beak, killing it instantly. This is lucky for the fish, because what comes next is pretty gory.

The squid uses its beak to rip out chunks of flesh, and shreds the meat into little bits with its radula.

Think before you swallow

Squids are not known for their patience. They would probably like to gulp down their food in big chunks and then rush back for seconds. But gobbling is a problem for cephalopods: it gives them a pain in the brain. A squid's brain is shaped like a doughnut, with the oesophagus (the swallowing tube) going through the hole in the middle. So the squid's food has to go through its brain to get to its stomach. To avoid a monster headache, the squid has to keep that radula moving, chain-sawing its food into little pieces and shoving the bits down its throat.

OOH... MY BRAIN...

HUMBOLDT OR JUMBO FLYING SQUID
(*Dosidicus gigas*)

It's no wonder Mexican fishermen call this critter the 'red devil'. Humboldt Squid are big, smart and very fierce. Weighing up to 150 kilograms (330 pounds), with a beak the size of an apple and suckers fringed with sharp saw-tooth points, these huge red squid are fierce predators. They eat many kinds of squids and large fish, including sharks. They will even eat each other!

These beasts can be close to 2 metres (6 feet) long. They are powerful swimmers, and even more powerful eating machines. Fishermen tell stories of Humboldt squids dragging down anything they can find in the water – even human beings. Nobody wants to risk falling overboard at night when the squids come to the surface to feed.

Divers tell of the eerie spectacle of huge squids rising from the depths, flashing red and white like strobe lights. This display is only the beginning. Divers have been grabbed and dragged under the water. They've had their equipment torn off and their skin ripped by the sharp hooks on the squids' suckers. Some divers use 'shark suits' or even specially made metal armour when swimming with these squids. But Australian cephalopod expert Dr Mark Norman says that you'd be crazy to use anything less than a protective shark cage.

Humboldt Squid usually inhabit waters from Chile up to California, in the warm Humboldt currents. In Mexico, fishing for jumbo squid is an important industry – more than 10 million of the squid are believed to live nearby.

Mysteriously, Humboldt Squid have started to appear stranded on beaches much further north, even as far as Alaska. The surprise visits may be due to the El Niño effect, with southern warmer water drifting north.

The octopus's secret weapon

The octopus's hunting technique is very different from the speedy strikes of the squid. Octopuses are stealth hunters that creep up on slow-moving prey like lobsters, crabs, shrimp, shellfish – and even other octopuses. You might think the octopus has it easy, with a complete seafood buffet available at its sucker-tips. But slow-moving prey aren't always a picnic. If you've ever tried to open an oyster with your bare hands, you'll know how difficult it can be. And those lobsters have pretty sharp claws . . .

Luckily for the octopus, it has a secret weapon: deadly saliva.

When an octopus grabs a tasty lobster, it needs to knock it out quickly, before the lobster can do too much damage with its claws. The octopus's beak is tucked deeper into its body than the squid's, so it needs to grab the lobster and get right on top of it before inflicting its deadly bite. Using its beak, the octopus pierces the lobster's shell, and then spits its poisonous saliva into the wound.

What happens next depends on the type of octopus. The poison used by some octopuses turns the lobster's flesh to a gloopy jelly, so the octopus can crack open the shell and slurp up the insides. Other octopuses use a poison that paralyses their prey. The prey may even remain alive and conscious but unable to move, while the octopus cracks the shell and pulls out the meat with its radula and its sucker-covered 'fingers'. Ouch. And you thought the squid attack was bad.

Some octopuses prefer shellfish, such as clams, which they open using another poisonous trick. These octopuses use their radula to drill a hole into the clam's shell, and then spit poison into the hole. The poison relaxes the clam's muscles, making it easy for the octopus to pull open the shell with its suckers and gobble up the morsel inside.

Eat in or take away?

Octopuses like to enjoy their meals in a safe, sheltered spot, to avoid being caught and eaten themselves. Some octopuses will go on little shopping expeditions. They pick up one animal and paralyse it, then carry it with their suckers while looking for another tasty dish. When the octopus's hands are full of paralysed critters, it carries the groceries home and has a complete meal. One way of spotting an octopus's hide-out is to look for its dirty dishes – the drilled or broken shells of its prey piled at the door.

An octopus stole my dinner!

People who fish for lobsters sometimes have the frustrating experience of being robbed by an octopus. An octopus can easily squeeze into a lobster trap and feast on the captive lobster at its leisure, protected from predators by the bars of the trap. When it has finished the octopus can scoot off home, leaving the empty shell – and a disappointed fisherman! An even nastier surprise is a half-eaten lobster. If an octopus has bitten your lobster but hasn't eaten it, you may find that the lobster's flesh has turned to a revolting jelly.

You are getting sleeeeeepy . . .

Probably the most bizarre hunting trick belongs to the Broadclub Cuttlefish (*Sepia latimanus*). This colourful creature can use the patterns on its skin to hypnotise its prey!

It does this by making dark bands of colour pulse rapidly along its body and arms. From the front, the cuttlefish's body looks like a weird, throbbing bullseye target, with the rings zooming into the middle. It is difficult to look away from this hypnotic optical trick. Before a fascinated fish can say 'Whoaaa, man, that is messing with my mind', the cuttlefish unleashes its feeding tentacles and grabs itself a meal.

8

BITE ME, I DARE YOU!

Still on the menu after 3000 years

The link between humans and cephalopods can be traced back to ancient times. Over 3000 years ago, Cretan artists decorated their vases and jugs with lifelike paintings of octopuses. Octopus images have also been found on ancient Greek coins and shields. This suggests that octopuses were important and valuable merchandise, and were also symbols of protection and good luck.

Today octopus, squid and cuttlefish are still an important part of Mediterranean cooking. Italy, France, Spain and Greece have many delicious cephalopod dishes – from calamari rings to pickled octopus tentacles, and even black cuttlefish-ink spaghetti.

Traditional tricks and traps

FUNKY OCTO APARTMENTS FREE!!

The ancient Greeks and Romans had some interesting tricks for catching octopuses. The most common was the water-jug trap, where a set of clay jugs was lowered into the water. These cosy containers would look like a perfect hiding spot for octopuses, which would curl up inside – ready to be hauled up to the surface. Local fishermen in parts of France still use a similar method today. When they empty an octopus out

HMM... CALL ME SUSPICIOUS, BUT...

of its jug, they quickly kill it in the traditional way – by biting its head just behind the eyes. This may sound horrible, but it is actually a quick and relatively painless death. Leaving an octopus to die slowly out of the water would be much worse.

Another old-style trick was to spread oil on the surface of the water to make it calm in that spot. When the water is calm, it is easier to see the octopuses lurking at the bottom. The ancient Greeks also had an ingenious way of detaching an octopus holding tightly to a rock. They found that waving a leaf of a certain plant, *Inula viscosa*, in front of the octopus would make the octopus release its grip. In modern-day Greece, local fishermen have discovered that waving a tobacco leaf near an octopus has the same effect.

A popular catch

Today, fishing for cephalopods is an enormous, multi-billion-dollar industry. At least 3 million tonnes of octopus, squid and cuttlefish are caught each year. Most of this catch is made up of two types of squids: inshore squids and flying squids caught in the northern Pacific Ocean. Octopuses make up about 10 per cent of the total cephalopod catch.

Commercial octopus fishers use large trawl nets rather than individual pots. Squids and cuttlefish are also caught in nets, or using a 'squid-jig' – a set of hooks baited with 'lures' designed to look like the squid's prey. Many squid-jigs also use lights as a way of attracting squid. The squid fishery in the Sea of Japan has so many glowing lures that it is actually visible from space!

Even though humans catch such enormous quantities of squids, they are not the biggest predator of cephalopods. Sperm whales still eat more squids each year than the total weight of fish consumed by humans. Now that's an appetite!

What's on the menu?
Some tasty cephalopod dishes from around the world ...

SPAIN

Chipirones en su tinta ★ Tiny octopuses cooked in their ink. Or try fried *chipirones* for a tasty *tapa* (snack).

ITALY

Calamari fritti ★ Ring-shaped slices of squid, crumbed and fried. The squid is first softened by soaking it in milk.

Seppia e il suo nero ★ Cuttlefish cooked in its ink. Cuttlefish ink is richer and tastier than squid ink. Both types of ink can also be used to make black spaghetti.

GREECE

Oktapodi toursi ★ Octopus marinated in olive oil, vinegar and herbs.

CROATIA

Dalmatinska salata od hobodnice ⋆ Octopus salad dressed with olive oil, red onions, lemon juice and garlic. Cooks recommend first boiling the octopus with some old wine corks to make it tender!

JAPAN

Ika sashimi ⋆ Thin slices of raw squid served with soy sauce and hot *wasabi* (horseradish).

Takoyaki ⋆ Fluffy baked balls of octopus, spring onions and egg batter, served with a special sauce and mayonnaise.

INDONESIA

Cumi-cumi isi ⋆ Squid stuffed with fish and macadamia nuts, simmered in coconut milk.

BURMA

Pyi-gying a kazun ywet ⋆ Squid cooked with dandelion leaves in soy sauce, lemon, chili and garlic.

one octopus you definitely don't want to eat...

What is it about Australia and poisonous animals? We've got a monster collection of poisonous snakes, we've got funnel-web and red-back spiders, and we even have the world's most poisonous fish, the stonefish. So it's no surprise that Australia is home to the world's most poisonous octopuses.

Blue-ringed octopuses are a group of small octopuses with distinctive bright blue rings on their bodies. When predators see the rings light up, they get the message, 'This little octopus packs a lot of poison'. Blue-rings have killed at least three people in Australia and Singapore, and there are reports of more than ten people who have been saved after a near-fatal bite. Blue-rings are shy animals, and have only bitten people after being pestered by them.

The Blue-ring's defence weapon is its toxic saliva. The saliva contains tetrodotoxin, a powerful nerve poison. With one small bite, the Blue-ring delivers enough poison to quickly paralyse a large animal or a person.

The toxin works by stopping the victim's nerves from carrying messages to their muscles. The strange (and creepy) thing about this paralysis is that it only affects muscles which you can usually control, like your arms, legs, mouth and so on. It doesn't stop your heart from beating or your eyes from seeing. Victims of a blue-ring bite can see and hear what is going on around them, but can't move or speak. Scary. After a short while the paralysis affects the muscles used for breathing, and the victim will die from lack of oxygen.

A bite victim can be saved by mouth-to-mouth resuscitation or an artificial breathing machine. It is important to seek help immediately if you think someone has been bitten by a Blue-ringed octopus.

Warning! Blue-ringed octopuses do not always have their blue rings on display. Like other octopuses, Blue-rings are masters of camouflage, and may look brown or sandy-coloured. To be safe, don't pick up, poke or pester any small octopuses in Australia or other Asian countries.

The artistic cephalopod

Chefs are not the only artists who make use of cephalopods. The famous Spanish painter and sculptor, Salvador Dali, once painted a portrait of the composer Beethoven using the ink of cuttlefish and squid. Dali was known for his bizarre artistic experiments. But in this case his choice of ink was not as strange as you might think.

In the 1700s and 1800s, artists used cuttlefish ink to make a reddish-brown drawing ink called sepia. '*Sepia*' is the scientific name for cuttlefish.

To make sepia, you had to remove the ink sacs from the cuttlefish, dry them and then grind them into a powder. The powder was then mixed with shellac (a resin which comes from the Lac beetle). Today there are many synthetic pigments which give the same red-brown sepia colour, although it is still possible to buy the real thing.

The pen is mightier than the squid.

A less artistic – but also useful – cuttlefish product is the chalky 'bone' which you may have found washed up on beaches. For pet birds like budgies and canaries, a 'cuttlebone' is a good source of calcium, and helps keep their beaks trim.

Police! Stop that squid!

Are squid being used to commit crimes? The answer is yes! Police in Peru have discovered that not all calamari is as innocent as it looks. In 2004, police seized a 25-tonne container of frozen squid about to leave Peru on its way to Mexico. Hidden inside the packets of squid were 700 kilograms (1500 pounds, or two-thirds of a ton) of illegal drugs worth millions of dollars. The criminals had covered the drugs in pepper and wrapped them in layers of plastic to throw sniffer dogs off the scent. But the police had already tracked the criminals' activities for months and were ready to make the arrest.

I wonder, though – if a squid had master-minded the plan, they might just have got away with it!

SOMETHING SMELLS FISHY...

NICKI GREENBERG has always been fascinated by strange creatures, especially the ones with goggly eyes. As a kid she kept pet snails which had hundreds of babies and then escaped into her bedroom. She still talks to snails in the street.

Like the octopus, Nicki is good at camouflage. She can often be found disguised as a lawyer, but on her days off she writes and illustrates comics. Nicki enjoys inventing her own strange creatures with goggly eyes, but she hasn't yet come up with anything as weird as the octopus. She likes to draw with the door closed so her two Bad Cats can't poke their whiskers into the ink – and so nobody can see the weird faces she makes while working.

Writing about squids and octopuses hasn't put Nicki off her favourite dish: crispy salt-and-pepper squid.

Thanks

Many thanks to Dr Mark Norman for his generous advice about cephalopods. And to my Big Squid, Stuart, and Little Squid, James, for listening to endless squid facts!

Nicki Greenberg

The publisher would like to thank Dr Mark Norman for checking the text, and the following for photographs used through the book:

Elisabeth Cölfen/istockphoto.com, pages i and 11

Dirk Diesel/istockphoto.com, pages viii–8 (cuttlefish)

Dr Steve O'Shea, pages 3 and 87 (Ocythoe tuberculata)

Dr Mark Norman, pages 7 and 58 (Architeuthis)

Dr James B. Wood, pages 7 (Sepia officinalis) and 8 (octopus suckers)

John Forsythe, pages 9 (Euprymna scolopes) and 27 (courting cuttlefish)

Nicki Greenberg, page 19 (Ram's Horn Squid shell)

Roger T. Hanlon, page 24 (Sepioteuthis lessoniana) and page 38 (Octopus vulgaris)

Jody Elliott/istockphoto.com, page 50

Dr George Jackson, page 61 (both photos Architeuthis)

Dan Schmitt/istockphoto.com, page 75

Thanks also to Tony Morelli at TONMO.com and all the helpful scientists we contacted whose work is displayed on the CephBase website.

Glossary

ammonia a chemical found in many squids' bodies. Ammonia helps squids to float, because it is lighter than water. Humans use ammonia in cleaning products – it has a sharp, unpleasant smell.

amphora an ancient Roman jug for storing water, wine and oil. The plural is 'amphorae'.

archaeologist a person who studies very old objects to learn about ancient civilisations

cephalopod the group of animals which includes squids, octopuses, cuttlefish and nautiluses

chromatophores tiny organs in a cephalopod's skin which allow it to change colour

enzymes chemicals which some squids use to produce their own light. There are many types of enzymes which cause different chemical reactions.

gladius the flexible 'bone' inside a squid's body

haemocyanin the copper pigment (colour) that makes cephalopods' blood blue

haemoglobin the iron pigment (colour) that makes humans' blood red

invertebrates animals without backbones. Cephalopods are invertebrates. So are insects, spiders, jellyfish, worms, prawns and other shellfish.

iridocytes reflective cells on a cephalopod's skin which give it a glittering blue/green colour

Kraken a legendary monster based on the giant squid

mantle the cephalopod's body, which is shaped like a bag or a tube

melanin the pigment that gives cephalopod ink its dark colour. Melanin is also found in human hair and skin. More melanin means darker hair or skin.

mollusc the group of animals which includes cephalopods, and also other animals like snails, slugs, oysters and clams

radula the cephalopod's 'tongue', which is covered with sharp, rasping teeth like a file

sepia the scientific name for cuttlefish, and the name of the artists' drawing ink made from cuttlefish ink

squid-jig a set of hooks used for catching squid

tetrodotoxin powerful nerve poison found in the saliva of Blue-ringed Octopuses

where to find out more

Books

Mark Norman and Amanda Reid, A *Guide to Squid, Cuttlefish and Octopuses of Australasia*, CSIRO Publishing with the Gould League of Victoria, Melbourne, 2000

Mark Norman and Helmut Debelius (illustrator), *Cephalopods – a World Guide*, Conchbooks, Hackenheim, 2000

Includes fabulous photos and an eye-witness account of a Humboldt Squid attack!

Websites

THE OCTOPUS NEWS MAGAZINE ONLINE

- www.tonmo.com

Includes photos sent in by readers and Kids-Parents-Teachers section with links and activities.

AUSTRALIAN CEPHALOPODS

- www.australiancephalopods.com

Highlights include video clips of an octopus running (very funny) and a cuttlefish showing its true colours.

IN SEARCH OF GIANT SQUID

- http://seawifs.gsfc.nasa.gov/squid.html

For teachers

TREE OF LIFE PROJECT

- www.tolweb.org

CEPHBASE

- www.cephbase.dal.ca

THE CEPHALOPOD PAGE

- http://is.dal.ca/~ceph/TCP/

Index